AMERICAN WAR BIOGRAPHIES

Ethan Allen

Karen Price Hossell

Heinemann Library
Chicago, Illinois

Designed by Heinemann Library
Page layout by Lisa Buckley
Maps by John Fleck and Heinemann Library
Photo research by Janet Lankford Moran
Printed and bound in China by South China Printing
   Company Limited

08 07 06 05 04
10 9 8 7 6 5 4 3 2 1

Library of Congress Cataloging-in-Publication Data
Price Hossell, Karen, 1957-
   Ethan Allen / Karen Price Hossell.
      p. cm. -- (American war biographies)
   Summary: A biography of Ethan Allen, the Revolutionary War
hero who led the Green Mountain Boys, a militia group he and
his brothers formed.
   Includes bibliographical references (p.) and index.
   ISBN 1-4034-5077-3 (lib. bdg.) -- ISBN 1-4034-5084-6 (pbk.)
   1. Allen, Ethan, 1738-1789--Juvenile literature. 2.
Soldiers--United States--Biography--Juvenile literature. 3.
Vermont--Militia--Biography--Juvenile literature. 4.
Vermont--History--Revolution, 1775-1783--Campaigns--Juvenile
literature. 5. United States--History--Revolution,
1775-1783--Campaigns--Juvenile literature. 6. Fort Ticonderoga
(N.Y.)--Capture, 1775--Juvenile literature. [1. Allen, Ethan,
1738-1789. 2. Soldiers. 3. Vermont--History--Revolution, 1775-
1783. 4. United States--History--Revolution, 1775-1783. 5. Fort
Ticonderoga (N.Y.)--Capture, 1775.] I. Title. II. Series.
   E207.A4P75 2004
   973.3'092--dc22

                              2003021784

Acknowledgments
The author and publisher are grateful to the following for
permission to reproduce photographs:
pp. 4, 7, 8, 12 Bettmann/Corbis; p. 5 Massachusetts Historical
Society, Boston, MA, USA/Bridgeman Art Library; p. 13 George
Wuerthner; p. 14 Heinemann Library; pp. 15, 18, 19 National
Archives and Records Administration; p. 24 New York Historical
Society, New York, USA/Bridgeman Art Library; pp. 27, 42 Corbis;
p. 29 The Granger Collection, New York; pp. 30, 33, 43 North
Wind Picture Archives; p. 31 Courtesy of Joncombe.com; p. 37
The Ira Allen House, Manchester, Vermont; p. 38 Courtesy of the
Provincial Collection, Heritage Branch/Culture and Sport
Secretariat/Province of New Brunswick; p. 40 David
Muench/Corbis

Cover photograph by Bettmann/Corbis

Special thanks to Gary Barr for his help in the preparation of
this book.

Every effort has been made to contact copyright holders of any
material reproduced in this book. Any omissions will be rectified
in subsequent printings if notice is given to the publisher.

Some words are shown in bold, **like
this.** You can find out what they mean
by looking in the glossary.

Contents

The Revolutionary War was fought by American **colonists** and the British. It officially began on April 19, 1775, in a battle at Lexington, Massachusetts, and officially ended in 1783.

Patriots and Loyalists

The American **colonies** were settled by Great Britain, and colonists were required to follow laws passed by Britain's top lawmaking body, called **Parliament.** In the early years of settlement, few colonists questioned this. But in the mid-1700s, Parliament began passing laws that angered many Americans. Parliament also began forcing colonists to pay taxes on many items. Because Great Britain did not allow Americans to be a part of Parliament, the colonists had no way to protest these laws except to write or speak out against them.

In the years leading up to the Revolutionary War, American colonists were becoming divided into two groups. One group, called **Loyalists,** believed that the colonies should remain a part of Great Britain. The other group was the **Patriots.**

Ethan Allen, like many colonists, was a Patriot. He believed that the British colonies in North America should be separate from Britain.

This glass bottle filled with tea leaves was part of the Boston Tea Party.

Many Patriots wanted to break all ties with Great Britain and form a nation that governed itself. Others felt at first that the colonies could remain tied to Great Britain, but that they should have more freedom.

The Boston Tea Party

Since they had little say in the way they were governed and no vote in Parliament, American colonists became frustrated with their inability to be heard by Great Britain. So in December 1773, American Patriots found a new way to get Britain's attention by staging what is called the Boston Tea Party in Boston, Massachusetts. To protest the tea tax, they boarded ships carrying tea and threw the tea into Boston Harbor. Parliament punished the Patriots for their actions by ordering British troops to move into Boston to make sure that nothing like this happened again. Then Parliament closed Boston Harbor, which meant that the British controlled which ships sailed in and out. By April of 1775, tensions had risen even more. Patriots who had once thought that the colonies could be content under British rule were changing their minds and agreeing with those who wanted complete independence from Great Britain.

One man who strongly believed in the ideas of freedom and independence was Ethan Allen. During the early years of the war, Allen fought bravely. He helped to capture an important fort, and he worked with leaders of the **Continental army** as their representative in Canada. But years before the war ended, he was captured by the British and held as a prisoner of war for more than two years.

5

1737 or 1738

January
Ethan Allen is born in Litchfield, Connecticut

1755

Allen goes to live with the Reverend Jonathan Lee

1757

August
Allen marches with militia to Fort William Henry

1762

Allen buys into an iron mine and marries

Ethan Allen was the oldest child of Joseph and Mary Allen. He was born on January 21, 1738—some sources say 1737—in Litchfield, Connecticut. In 1740 his father moved the family to Cornwall, Connecticut. At the time, Cornwall was considered the **frontier.** It was a small village with few settlers.

Education

Because Cornwall was so small, it did not even have a school. But Ethan's parents made sure he learned whatever they could teach him. He learned how to read from two books, the Bible and another book called *Lives,* a history written by a Roman named Plutarch in the beginning of the second century C.E.

Ethan was a quick learner. He was interested in many things and tried to learn whatever he could. He also spent a lot of time helping his father on the family farm. It was hard work, because the Connecticut winters were harsh and the soil was poor.

The Allens thought that Ethan would do well in college, so early in 1755, when he was seventeen, they sent him to live with the Reverend Jonathan Lee, a distant relative. The plan was for Reverend Lee to teach Ethan everything he needed to know to get into Yale College, which is now Yale University. But just before he started, Ethan had to return home when his father suddenly died in April of 1755. After his father's death, Ethan became the oldest male in the family, and with that role came much responsibility. He had to find a way to take care of his mother and his seven

The French and Indian War, also called the Seven Years' War, was fought in North America from 1754 to 1763. The war was fought between the French and the British for land and trade rights in North America.

younger brothers and sisters. With their mother's and Ethan's guidance, the Allens all pitched in to keep the family farm going.

The French and Indian War

In 1754 the **French and Indian War** began in the **colonies** over ownership of land in the western part of Pennsylvania and the Ohio River Valley. On one side of the war were the French, who persuaded many Native Americans to help them fight. On the other side were the British and the American **colonists.** By 1757, Ethan felt that he was old enough to join in the fighting. He had already joined the local **militia,** and in August of 1757, they had learned that the French were planning to capture Fort William Henry, near Lake George, New York. Ethan's **militia** quickly began the 100-mile (160-kilometer) march to the fort to help defend it against the French. By the time they arrived, however, the French had already seized the fort, so the militia marched back home.

Men fighting during the Revolutionary War usually carried muskets with which to defend themselves.

Mining

Ethan Allen kept his eye out for ways to make money in the New England **frontier.** In 1762 he and a few other men bought water and timber rights to Tohconnick Mountain. This meant that they could explore the mountain and keep what they found. For years people had said that the mountain contained lots of iron ore, and Allen and his partners decided to find out for sure. It turns out their hunch was right. They found lots of iron ore, which was used to make cannons and **muskets** during the Revolutionary War, among other things.

That same year, Allen married a woman he had been friends with for several years. Her name was Mary Brownson. Mary was six years older than Ethan, but the two got along well. After they married Allen sold his share of the iron **forge** and moved to Salisbury, Connecticut. In Salisbury he became friends with Dr. Thomas Young. The two men enjoyed discussing politics and religion, and they started to write a book together. When Ethan had the opportunity to buy a lead mine in Northhampton, Connecticut, he moved his family there. But the lead mine was not as successful as the iron mine.

Getting into arguments

Ethan Allen ran into trouble in Northhampton. Most of the people who lived there were very religious, but Allen was not. He had thought about and questioned religion for years, and he had many arguments with townspeople over their religious views. Local church leaders visited Allen and asked him to stop arguing with people in shops and **taverns** and on the streets, but he would not. So in July 1767, the people of Northhampton voted to ask the Allens to leave town. The family returned to Salisbury. To make money, Ethan and his brother Levi started traveling through the Berkshire Mountains, hunting for beaver and other animals. They sold the furs in the general store owned by their brother Heman. The family worked together to get things and make a living. Allen's other brothers and sisters did their part by working on the family farm in Cornwall.

Family ties

Even though they were all now adults, the Allen family stuck together. When his sister became very ill in 1769, Allen's entire family went to Goshen, Connecticut, to be with her. She died a year later, and soon after Allen's mother had a stroke. But the family stayed together, and soon they all decided to move to the New Hampshire Grants.

3 The New Hampshire Grants

1770

The Allen family moves to the New Hampshire Grants

1774

A Brief Narrative of the Proceedings of the Government of New York is published

In 1763 the **French and Indian War** ended. France lost the war and gave up rights to Canada and to all land east of the Mississippi River. Now that there was peace, people felt more comfortable moving around and settling in other parts of the country. One place some people settled was called the New Hampshire Grants. This land was north of New York and west of New Hampshire, and it eventually became the state of Vermont. Ethan Allen had roamed through the area while hunting. He thought it would be a good idea for the entire Allen family to move to the Grants. He also thought that if he bought land cheaply there, before other settlers came in, he could sell it at a profit as people moved in and wanted land. He moved his entire family, including his brothers and sisters and their families, to the Green Mountains in the New Hampshire Grants in 1770. In 1772 he sold the family's farm in Cornwall.

There was a problem with the land in the New Hampshire Grants, however, because more than one group claimed it. In colonial times, the **boundaries** between one **colony** and another were uncertain. Some borders were based on

Publishing a book

In his work to defend landowners in the New Hampshire Grants, Ethan Allen spent a great deal of time studying ancient charters and the histories of the colonies. With the knowledge he gained, he wrote a book called *A Brief Narrative of the Proceedings of the Government of New York*. The book is more than 200 pages long and was published in 1774. He wrote four other books about this topic as well.

old **charters** drawn up by whatever British ruler was on the throne at the time the colony was settled. Because there were no accurate maps of North America in those days, the charters were vague. They might say, for example, that the border of a colony extended from the Atlantic Ocean to the Pacific Ocean. People knew about both oceans but had no idea that thousands of miles of land lay between them. If the United States today had the borders laid out in those old charters, the state of Virginia would extend all the way from the shores of the Atlantic to the shores of the Pacific.

Confusing charters

It was not just that boundaries and land measurements were not exact. Sometimes there were two charters giving the same plot of land to two different people or groups of people. In the 1600s, for example, the English King Charles II gave his brother, the Duke of York, a plot of land to be called New York. The problem was that the charters of Massachusetts and Connecticut, which were older than the charter drawn up by Charles II, said that those colonies extended all the way to the Pacific Ocean. That meant that all land to the west, including New York, belonged to them. Besides the confusion about charters, there was no official power in the American colonies to oversee the buying and selling of land, or to **survey** land.

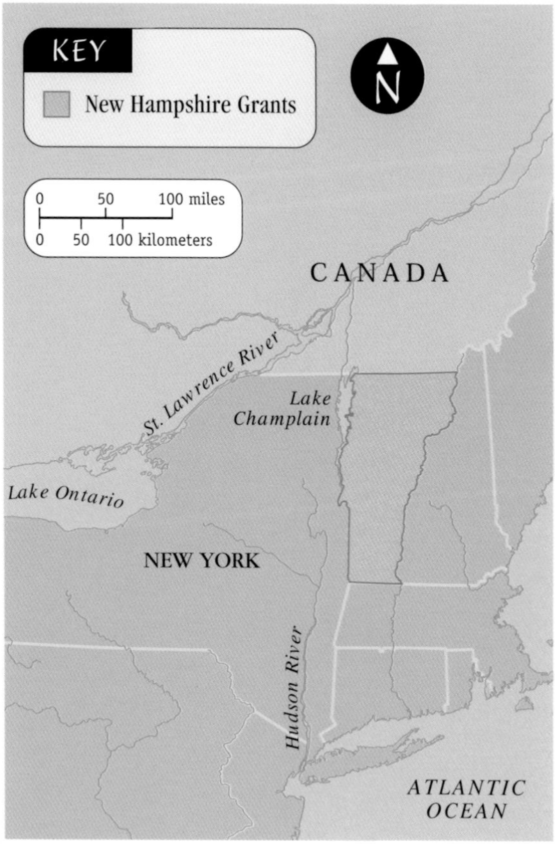

KEY

New Hampshire Grants

0   50   100 miles
0   50   100 kilometers

CANADA

St. Lawrence River

Lake Champlain

Lake Ontario

NEW YORK

Hudson River

ATLANTIC OCEAN

The New Hampshire Grants are shown here. The area is now the state of Vermont. In Allen's time, boundaries of specific territories were often difficult to know with any certainty.

Eventually New York, Massachusetts, and Connecticut came to an agreement over **boundaries.** But settlers in New Hampshire also claimed some of the land that New York claimed, and confusion arose. Sometimes settlers in the New Hampshire Grants would build a home and start a farm, then be forced off the land, or **evicted,** by officials from New York. That is what was happening when Ethan Allen and his family moved to the Grants.

Charles II was King of England from 1660 to 1685. He gave the land that became New York to his brother, the Duke of York.

When Ethan Allen was alive, the Onion River was also known as the French River. This is because it had been used by the French and the Native Americans between 1704 and 1759 as a route to areas in Massachusetts.

Allen had been named to help defend those who were being evicted. Soon, the Allens and other families in the region decided to start fighting back against the New Yorkers. They formed a **militia** they called the Green Mountain Boys.

The Onion River Company

Not long after the Allens settled in the New Hampshire Grants, they formed the Onion River Company, named after a nearby river. The company was formed to purchase land, then resell it at a profit. The members of the company were Ethan Allen, his brothers Ira, Heman, and Zimry, and their friend Remember Baker, who later went with Allen when he invaded Fort Ticonderoga. The company owned about 77,000 acres of land but had difficulty making a profit because of the troubles with New York. Today, the Onion River is called the Winooski River.

4 The Green Mountain Boys

1770

The Green
Mountain Boys
militia is formed

The Green Mountain Boys were organized in 1770. Ethan Allen was chosen to lead the **militia,** which was made up of five separate companies. Because of his work in local politics, Allen had a reputation as a strong leader. He was more well-read than most settlers, and he was a good speaker. By most accounts, he was more than 6 feet (1.8 meters) tall, which was unusual in those days. As colonel-commandant of the Green Mountain Boys, Allen wore a flashy uniform and carried a large sword.

Shamings

But the sword was just for show. The Green Mountain Boys never killed anyone. Instead, the Green Mountain Boys used **tactics** such as threats and what were called shamings. One example of a shaming occurred when a man named Dr. Samuel Adams, who lived in the New Hampshire Grants, began to defend New York and speak out against the Green Mountain Boys. He was told to stop encouraging settlers to buy land through New York claims, but he said that he was free to talk about anything he liked. He also said that he would use the pistols he carried on any man who tried to stop him. The Green Mountain Boys responded by picking up Dr. Adams and carrying him to the **tavern** where they often held their meetings. The tavern's sign was on a pole that was 25 feet high and featured a large stuffed wildcat with large teeth. The cat was positioned

This is the flag of the Green Mountain Boys militia.

so that it faced New York. The Green Mountain Boys sat the doctor in a chair, tied him to the chair, and lifted the chair to the top of the sign. They left the doctor there for two hours. During that time a crowd of people stood below and made fun of him. The Green Mountain Boys did use more violent tactics, as well. Sometimes they would severely whip someone, and a few times they burned down cabins and crops.

George Washington was the first president of the United States. He fought on the side of the **colonists** during the Revolutionary War.

A fierce reputation

The reputation of the Green Mountain Boys was fierce. Often, when men were sent to force settlers off their land, the Green Mountain Boys only had to get word out that they were on their way to fight and their enemies would run. Many New Yorkers also feared Ethan Allen himself, even though most of them had never met him. When the Green Mountain Boys captured an official, they would put him on trial. Allen would lead the trial, and the offender was always found guilty. The punishment would usually be to tie the offender to a tree and beat him with sticks.

In 1775 Ethan Allen and the Green Mountain Boys would become known far and wide for more than their fierce acts in the New Hampshire Grants. They became known for their acts of bravery when they took part in the capture of a fort that was about 70 miles away from Allen's home in Bennington, Vermont. This capture was one of the first actions in the Revolutionary War.

5   The Capture of Fort Ticonderoga

Fort Ticonderoga was at the southern tip of Lake Champlain in New York and was occupied by British troops. Lake Champlain is between New York and Vermont, but its northernmost tip is in Canada, and Canada was a British territory. While the American **colonies** were also ruled by the British, by 1775 **colonists** were seeking independence. If American troops could capture Fort Ticonderoga, they figured it would show the British that they were serious about winning their freedom. Also, after the battles of Lexington and Concord in April of 1775, many Americans thought British troops would sail down Lake Champlain into New York to fight against the **Patriots.** If the Patriots held the fort, they could stop British ships that were trying to move into the colonies.

Because troubles had been brewing in the colonies for some time, each colony had agreed to set up a **committee of correspondence.** Members of the committees wrote letters to the other committees telling them how things were going in their colonies. In the letters they might mention what British officials were doing in their towns, or what kinds of preparations they were making for a possible war. A few weeks before the Battle of Lexington, the Massachusetts Committee of Correspondence decided to send representatives into Canada. They were to find out how Canadians felt about the Americans seeking independence from Great Britain. They discovered that the Canadians supported American independence and the capture of Fort Ticonderoga by the colonists. The Americans knew there were cannons, ammunition, and other weapons at the fort that Patriot soldiers could use to fight the British.

Fort Ticonderoga protected an important water route into New York, which made it important for both the British and Americans.

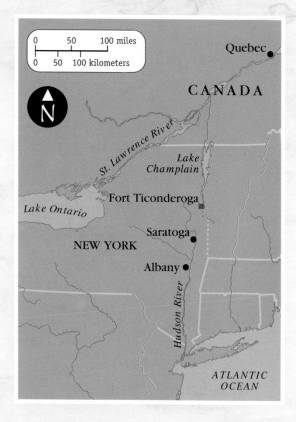

While the Massachusetts committee was coming up with a plan to seize the fort, a similar plan was being arranged in Connecticut. Several members of the colony's government met secretly to discuss the capture of the fort. They managed to put together $1,000 to help pay for the expedition to Ticonderoga, and they began to **recruit** men to do the job. They visited the **militia** groups in the area, including the Green Mountain Boys.

The Green Mountain Boys were eager to get involved in the expedition to Fort Ticonderoga. Because of his reputation as a good leader, the Connecticut committee chose Ethan Allen to lead the expedition. He was instructed to lead his men to Shoreham, a town that was directly across the lake from Ticonderoga. Some of his men were to go to another small settlement to get boats. The two groups would meet up and use the boats to sail across the lake. They would **ambush** the fort and capture it for the Americans.

As Allen was leading his band of 270 men to Fort Ticonderoga, he learned that another group of militiamen, led by Colonel Benedict Arnold, was on the same mission. While Allen and his men had been sent to the fort by the committee from Connecticut, Arnold had been sent by the Massachusetts committee. On May 7 the two leaders met at Castleton, Vermont, to come up with a plan that would allow each man to complete his mission.

Arnold believed that as an officer in the **Continental army**, he should be the one to lead. But the Green Mountain Boys declared that they would follow no one but Allen. The two men argued for a while over who should lead, then decided to join forces and command as equals.

A young boy helps

After the troops reached Shoreham, Allen asked a local farmer if he knew anyone who could explain the layout of the fort. The farmer said that his

Ethan Allen informs the British commander of Fort Ticonderoga that the fort has been captured by the **colonists** and that he should surrender his garrison.

young son, Nathan Beman, had visited the fort many times to play with the children of soldiers who lived there. The farmer agreed to allow his son to go along as the Americans attacked the fort. Allen and Arnold asked Nathan many questions before they set out, and then used the young boy as their guide once they reached the fort.

The ambush

In the middle of the night on May 10, 1775, the troops began crossing Lake Champlain. Because they had so few boats, only 83 men managed to make it to Ticonderoga. Instead of waiting for all of the men to cross, Allen and Arnold decided they should attack, since dawn would soon come.

The attack caught all at the fort by surprise. Because news traveled so slowly in those days, the soldiers inside the fort did not even know

Benedict Arnold

During the early years of the Revolutionary War, Benedict Arnold was a well-respected general. Many people, including General George Washington, trusted Arnold and looked to him for leadership on the battlefield. But in 1779, Arnold turned away from the **Patriot** cause and became a spy for the British. When his disloyalty was discovered, he escaped to England, where he died in 1801.

about the battles at Lexington and Concord. They did not realize that a war had begun, so they had only one man guarding the entryway. Walking side by side, Allen and Arnold led their men to the gate. They threatened to kill the guard, who quickly let them inside. The **militiamen** then entered the fort. Nathan knew exactly where Captain Delaplace, the man in charge of the fort, was sleeping, and he led Allen and Arnold there. The two leaders demanded that the captain surrender the fort to them. Because he had just woken up—it was about four o'clock in the morning by that time—Captain Delaplace was confused at first. He did not quite understand who these men were and why they were attacking the fort. When Allen raised his sword, however, the captain surrendered. Later, Benedict Arnold and Ethan Allen disagreed over exactly what had happened at the fort, but there is no question that the fort was taken without a drop of blood being shed.

The Americans rounded up all the British soldiers and took them and their families as prisoners of war. They captured 42 soldiers, plus their wives and children. The Americans also seized the cannons and other weapons at the fort. Because Fort Ticonderoga had not been used for combat since the **French and Indian War**, many of the cannons were old and rusty. Some were even half-buried under dirt, and some had slid or been pushed into the lake. But the Americans gathered all they could and readied them for battle. Later, these were taken to Boston by troops led by Colonel Henry Knox. There, the cannons were placed on Dorchester Heights, an area high above the city, and used against the British.

Arnold and Allen argue

According to a history book published in 1909, after the ambush at Fort Ticonderoga, Nathan Beman saw Arnold and Allen arguing. Beman said that at one point, Arnold became so upset with Ethan Allen that he knocked Allen's hat from his head and into the mud.

On May 11, the day after the **ambush,** a band of Americans led by Green Mountain Boy Colonel Seth Warner captured a smaller fort, called Fort Amherst, at nearby Crown Point. They found about 100 more cannons at the fort. Only a few British soldiers were defending the crumbling fort at the time.

Arnold's accusations

Later, Colonel Arnold harshly criticized the behavior of the Green Mountain Boys during the raid on Fort Ticonderoga. He claimed that many of Allen's men had disappeared before the ambush was completed. He also accused the Green Mountain Boys of stealing items they had found in the fort. Many historians agree with Arnold's claim that Ethan Allen and his men unfairly took credit for doing most of the work during the raid. Whatever the facts, Ethan Allen never gave Benedict Arnold and his troops much credit for their part in the mission.

An important event

The capture of Forts Ticonderoga and Amherst was the first important event of the American Revolution. It proved to the British that the Americans could outsmart them, and it showed Americans that they had a chance to defeat the British. Besides gaining important forts for the Americans, the captures also provided renewed confidence for **Patriots** as they began their fight for freedom.

Fort Carillon

In 1759, British Lord Jeffery Amherst captured Fort Ticonderoga from the French. At the time, the fort was named Carillon. Amherst renamed it Ticonderoga, which is from the Iroquois word meaning "land between the waters." The British destroyed much of the fort during their invasion. They rebuilt the star-shaped fort and placed around its outside a ring called an abatis, which was a ditch filled with upright sharpened sticks and small trees. At the end of the French and Indian War in 1763, Fort Ticonderoga officially became British territory.

The confidence Allen's and Arnold's troops gained with the capture of Forts Ticonderoga and Amherst made them think of other ways to attack the British. As they continued to occupy Fort Ticonderoga, Allen and Arnold decided to sail to Fort St. John's in Quebec, Canada. On the way they would capture a British **sloop** armed with sixteen guns.

Fort St. John's

Some of the soldiers had already gone to a nearby settlement called Skenesborough to get boats. While they were there they had seized a **schooner** and other smaller boats. In keeping with their goal for the **colonies**, they renamed the schooner *Liberty*. Because Benedict Arnold had experience sailing ships, he was made commander of the mission to Fort St. John's. Arnold and his men sailed in the *Liberty,* and Allen and his men were to follow in some of the smaller boats.

On May 15, 1775, Arnold came within 30 miles (48 kilometers) of the British sloop. He ordered his men into the smaller boats that were aboard *Liberty*. The American sailors quietly rowed up to the sloop and quickly captured it, taking thirteen prisoners. Later, the sloop was renamed *Enterprise.* They sailed the sloop to Fort St. John's and easily captured that as well. On the voyage back to Ticonderoga, they ran into Allen's men sailing in their smaller boats. Allen and Arnold met and decided that Allen would go to Fort St. John's and remain there, holding it for the Americans. But as they approached St. John's, Allen and

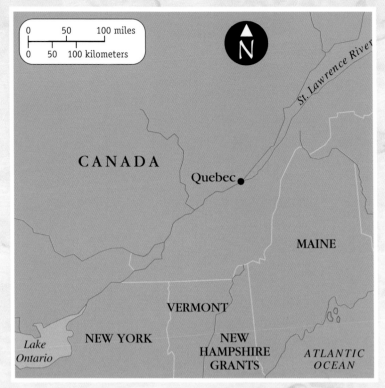

St. John's Fort and the city of Quebec were located at an important spot, controlling a point on the St. Lawrence River.

his troops were attacked by more than 200 British soldiers who had just arrived as **reinforcements,** so they fled back to Fort Ticonderoga.

Not long after, about 600 reinforcements came from Connecticut to help keep Fort Ticonderoga and Fort Amherst in American hands. The troops were led by Colonel Hinman. He informed Allen and Arnold that orders from home were for Allen to stay at Ticonderoga, and Arnold to remain with his men at Crown Point. Hinman said that he had been charged with taking over the entire operation at the two forts.

Plan to invade Canada

Ethan Allen knew that there were many **Loyalists** in Canada, and that the Americans had a better chance of winning independence if they stopped the Loyalist party there. He also knew that if the Americans attacked Canada,

During the Revolutionary War, **schooners** would have looked like this.

many of the British forces that were occupying Boston would rush to Canada to fight them. While at Ticonderoga, Allen came up with a plan to invade Canada. He sent a letter outlining his plan to the **Continental Congress.** In his letter, Allen wrote that "I would lay my life on it, that with fifteen hundred men I could take Montreal." He went on to write that once Montreal was taken, it would not be too difficult to capture the Canadian city of Quebec. However, Congress did not think the invasion of Canada was a good idea at the time. Congress thought it important to remain as friendly as possible with the people of Canada.

Allen speaks to Congress

Because Colonel Hinman was now in charge at Ticonderoga, Ethan Allen was free to go to Philadelphia to speak to the Continental Congress. He asked the congressmen to pay his **militiamen** for their work, and Congress agreed to do so. Because they had been so successful in their mission, Congress also voted to include the Green Mountain Boys in the official army of the **colonies,** called the **Continental army.** Then Congress told Allen and Warner to go to New York's Congress to ask their permission to enlarge the Green Mountain Boys militia. They were told to go to New York because that state claimed much of the land that was home to the Green Mountain Boys. But when Allen and Warner traveled to New York and requested to be received by Congress, they were at first refused. Many in the Congress saw them as outlaws for their behavior toward the people of New York.

However, after much discussion, the New York Congress allowed Allen and Warner into its chambers. The two men explained that the Continental Congress had suggested that they ask New York for permission to raise more troops for the Green Mountain Boys. The New York Congress agreed that they could **recruit** up to 500 men.

Returning home

Allen and his second-in-command, Seth Warner, then went back to the New Hampshire Grants to recruit more members for the Green Mountain Boys. While Allen had been the commander of the militia, back home Seth Warner was voted to lead the new army. Allen claimed that he was not selected because the older settlers, who made up most of the voters, saw him as someone who was too headstrong and who had wild ideas.

Allen goes to Canada

Allen then went back to Fort Ticonderoga. There, he volunteered his services however they could best be used. While earlier Congress had turned down Allen's plan for invading Canada, now many leaders were beginning to think it might be a good idea. General Philip Schuyler, who was in charge of the **Continental army** troops in the north, decided to send Allen to Canada to see how the Canadians felt about the Americans invading British posts there. Schuyler gave Allen a letter addressed to the people of Canada, telling them that Americans considered them to be friends and that the invasion would be against the British, not the Canadian people. Most Canadians were not British—they were either native peoples or French. They welcomed Allen and told him that they would join in the fight for freedom, although they feared there would not be enough of them to win over the British. When Allen returned eight days later, he told General Schuyler that the Canadian people would join with the Americans if they brought in a large force. Because Schuyler had become ill, another general, Richard Montgomery, was put in charge of the mission to Canada. He sent Allen back to Canada to **recruit** troops to help in the attack.

Allen recruited about 100 troops in Canada. While there, he met up with Major John Brown from the **Continental army,** who talked Allen into joining with him to attack Montreal. Brown and his men would attack Montreal from the north, and Allen and his men would attack from the south.

The invasion fails

On the night of September 24, Allen and his men sailed across the St. Lawrence River to just outside Montreal. Then they waited for the signal Brown was supposed to give to let them know it was time to attack. But the signal never came because Brown and his army had not been able to cross the river. While they were waiting, Allen's men captured a British soldier who was on his way to Montreal. But the man escaped and ran to the city to warn the people there about the planned attack.

As a result of his warning, about 300 soldiers came from Montreal to face Allen's army of 110 men. After a two-hour fight, during which many of his men **deserted,** Allen was forced to surrender. He and the other 38 men who had remained with him were taken prisoner by the British. By that time, it was September 25, 1775. For the next two years and seven months, Ethan Allen was held captive by the British.

Fort St. John's

Allen's plan to hold Fort St. John's in May 1775 failed. However, on November 2, 1775, after a long **siege** by American troops led by General Montgomery, the British surrendered the fort.

This is the gate at Fort St. John's. Arnold took control of the fort's guns, but British **reinforcements** arrived before Allen could take hold of the fort.

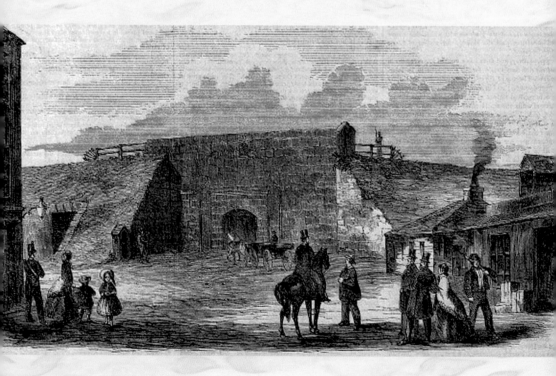

7   Prisoner of War

After his arrest, Allen was taken to Montreal to meet with General Prescott of the British army. Because of his actions at the capture of Fort Ticonderoga, Prescott knew who Allen was and scolded him for taking the fort. While many American **Patriots** were claiming an identity separate from the Great Britain, Prescott saw Allen as a rebel, someone who went against British authority. After his release in 1778 Allen wrote a book called *The Narrative of Colonel Ethan Allen*, which tells the story of his capture and imprisonment. In the book, Allen writes that Prescott "shook his cane over my head, calling many hard names, among which he frequently used the word rebel, and put himself in a great rage." After threatening to kill Allen and some of the Canadians who had fought with him, the General decided instead to imprison them on a **schooner.** The schooner was called the *Gaspee*.

Put in irons

Allen was put in handcuffs and leg irons. They prevented him from walking fast or escaping. The leg irons weighed about thirty pounds. He wrote that "The irons were so close upon my ancles, that I could not lie down in any other manner than on my back, I was put into the lowest and most wretched part of the vessel, where I got the favour of a chest to sit on, the same answered for my bed at night . . ." Because of the handcuffs and leg irons, it was hard for Allen to lie down and sleep. He asked to have them loosened, but the officers on the ship refused. Allen was a target for the officers' hatred for Patriots, and while he was on the ship, officers often came down to **harass** him.

Allen was aboard the *Gaspee* for about six weeks. During that time, he shouted at his captors and wrote letters to British generals complaining about his treatment. He reminded the generals that when he had taken prisoners at Ticonderoga, he treated them fairly. His letters received no response. Allen became so frustrated with his treatment that he said that he actually used his teeth to twist off a nail from his irons. His captors responded to this by replacing the nail with a padlock.

Sailing to England

Later, Allen was removed from the *Gaspee* and taken to another ship where his irons were removed and he was treated more fairly. However, he was there for only eight or nine days. Allen was then moved to the *Adamant*, a ship used to take prisoners to England. In England, Allen

Here, Ethan Allen sits in irons as a prisoner of war.

was to be tried for **treason.** He writes that they were put in "A small place in the vessel, enclosed with white-oak plank . . . I should imagine it was no more than twenty feet one way, and twenty the other. Into this place we were all, to the number of thirty-four, thrust and hand-cuffed." The prisoners were provided with large tubs to use as toilets, and they were forced to remain in these close quarters for the entire voyage. Allen complained that they were given very little water and that while many of them felt sick during the voyage, no one died.

The voyage lasted about forty days. During that time, Allen was sometimes visited by members of the ship's crew, who would **taunt** him and tell him that when he arrived in England, he would be hanged. One crew member even spit in Allen's face.

American prisoners during the Revolutionary War were kept in this prison ship in New York harbor.

Pendennis Castle was originally built by Henry VIII, King of England from 1509-1547.

Pendennis Castle

When the prisoners walked off the ship in England, they were greeted by a large crowd of people who were curious about these American rebels. The prisoners were taken to Pendennis Castle, which is at the western end of England. Meanwhile, **Parliament** debated whether to execute Allen or just keep him prisoner.

While at Pendennis, Allen and the other prisoners were treated well. Many curious people came to the castle to look at the prisoners. Some came to visit Allen in his cell, while others waited outside for Allen and the other prisoners to be

Prisoner of war exchanges

Prisoner of war exchanges during the Revolutionary War were worked out particularly when officers were being held prisoner. Because each side needed the knowledge and experience the officers had to help them win the war, they would **negotiate** terms to get the officers released. The terms would be in writing and could be somewhat complicated. They could sometimes resemble a game—for example, the terms might say that ten "common" prisoners could be exchanged for one colonel, or forty prisoners for a colonel and a general.

Prisoners of war during the Revolutionary War

Although Allen was not always treated well as a prisoner of war, most prisoners of war during the Revolution were treated even worse. In fact, the British army held thousands of Americans as prisoners of war. They were kept on about sixteen old ships in the East River in New York City, and often as many as 1,000 men were packed on board each ship. Many died during their imprisonment and were buried in mass graves. Many of the graves were in Brooklyn, New York, because the British occupied that area. There was little air on the ships because the portholes were blocked up, leaving only small holes for air to pass through. One prisoner, Robert Sheffield of Connecticut, managed to escape from a prison ship and later wrote that the prisoners were "swearing . . . crying, praying and wringing their hands, and stalking about like ghosts; others delirious [mad], raving and storming; some groaning and dying—all panting for breath; some dead and corrupting [decaying]—air so foul at times that a lamp could not be kept burning, by reason of which the boys were not missed till they had been dead ten days." Prisoners were released if they agreed to join the British army and fight against the Americans, or if they were part of a prisoner exchange. Historians estimate that about 11,500 men died aboard these ships. In contrast, 4,435 Americans died in battle during the Revolution.

taken outdoors for exercise and fresh air. Allen wrote that he often lectured the visitors about the foolishness of Great Britain in trying to conquer the American **colonies.**

Back to America

Allen did not have to face trial, and probably death, for **treason** after all. England's King George III decided not to put Allen on trial or have him hanged. He feared that the American army would do the same in revenge to British officers it had captured. So Allen and some other prisoners were put back on a ship named the *Solebay* and sent back to the colonies. On the return voyage, the *Solebay* stopped at a cove near Cork, Ireland, for supplies. Some businessmen in Cork had heard that American prisoners, including the famous Ethan Allen, were on board the ship. They sent cloth and clothing to all the prisoners. Allen received enough cloth to make two suits, eight shirts, stockings, two hats, and two pairs of shoes. The Irishmen also brought wine, sugar, coffee, tea, chocolate, and many kinds of food for Allen and the other prisoners to enjoy on their voyage. One man even gave Allen money. Later, however, the ship's captain took away the liquor, tea, and sugar. The Irishmen most likely gave the gifts because they and their countrymen had been under British rule for years and understood the American desire for independence.

The *Solebay* reached the coast of North Carolina on May 3, 1776. After that, Allen remained imprisoned on a series of ships. They sailed up and down the American coast and also anchored off Halifax, Nova Scotia. Sometimes Allen was treated well. At least once, he was invited to join the captain for dinner. Other times he thought the ship's captain and crew

George III was King of England during the Revolutionary War. He is shown here in his special royal clothing.

mistreated him. During his entire imprisonment, Allen wrote letters to the **Continental Congress,** to the captains of the ships he was on, and to doctors when other prisoners became sick and needed help.

In November of 1776 Allen was given **parole,** which meant he could leave the ship. He was allowed to live in New York City, which at the time was occupied by the British. However, he could not leave the city, and guards were placed near him to make sure he did not. On January 22, 1777, Allen and other American prisoners were taken to western Long Island, New York, and imprisoned there. He was again allowed to roam the streets and visit **taverns** and shops. However, on August 25, 1777, he was arrested for violating his parole and put into what he called "a lonely apartment." Allen remained there until May 3, 1778, when he was exchanged for a British prisoner and sent back to the American army. After his release, he wrote that he was "in a transport of joy, landed on liberty ground, and as I advanced into the country, received the acclamations of a grateful people."

A free man

One of the first things Allen did after his release was go to see General George Washington at his headquarters at Valley Forge, Pennsylvania. He wanted to thank General Washington for working out the prisoner exchange. All along the way on his journey from New York to Valley Forge, Allen met people who had heard of his imprisonment and who welcomed him back to America. While meeting with Washington, Allen offered his services to the

Ethan Allen's narrative

When Ethan Allen wrote and published his story of his imprisonment, *The Narrative of Colonel Ethan Allen,* many people were impressed by the bravery he claimed to have shown. But most modern historians believe that Allen exaggerated his actions in the narrative to make himself look better. Still, except for a few brief mentions in old books, the narrative is the only record we have of what happened to Allen.

Scurvy

One disease suffered by sailors before and during Allen's time was scurvy. Sailors who got scurvy had bleeding and spongy gums, were tired and achy, bruised easily, and sometimes bled from their fingertips. By the 1800s, many sailors knew that fresh fruits and vegetables helped to protect them against scurvy. Today, we know that this is because scurvy is caused by a lack of vitamin C, which is plentiful in fruits and vegetables. Allen wrote that when his prison ship was off the coast of Halifax, Nova Scotia, crew members were treated for scurvy this way:

We arrived at Halifax not far from the middle of June, where the ship's crew, which was infested with scurvy, were taken on shore, and shallow trenches dug, into which they were put, and partly covered with earth; indeed, every proper measure was taken for their relief.

He writes that not long after, "one of the men almost dead of the scurvy, lay by the side of the **sloop,** and a canoe of Indians coming by, he purchased two quarts of strawberries, and eat them at once, and it almost cured him." The man tried to get more strawberries for the other sick sailors but could not find any.

Continental army. But although the Continental Congress rewarded Allen's bravery in the battle at Montreal by promoting him to the rank of **brevet colonel,** Allen never rejoined the army. His role in the American Revolution was over.

Allen left Valley Forge and went to Bennington, where he met with the Green Mountain Boys. He wrote that they were surprised, because they had not heard of his release. Some people even thought he was dead. In Bennington, cannons were fired to celebrate Allen's release. Now that he was back home, Allen quickly became involved in the troubles that continued in Vermont.

1776

July 4
Congress announces
it has declared
independence from
Great Britain

1777

January 15
The New Hampshire
Grants declare
themselves to be a
free and
independent state

1780

March 30
Allen receives the
first letter from
British General
Robinson; the
general tries to get
Allen and Vermont
to join the British
cause; Allen does
not answer but
enters into
negotiations with
General Haldimand
in Canada
March 9

1781

Allen sends two
letters from
Robinson to
Congress so they
can see what is
going on

While Ethan Allen had been a prisoner of war, the people of the New Hampshire Grants had been busy. On July 4, 1776, the **Continental Congress** had made public the Declaration of Independence, which declared the American **colonies** to be free and independent states, no longer under British rule. The people of the New Hampshire Grants had always been independent people, and the Declaration of Independence inspired them to declare their own independence officially. On January 15, 1777, they announced that the region of the Grants was now a free and independent state. At first state leaders called their state New Connecticut. Soon, though, it was changed to Vermont. One of the men who was involved in the formation of Vermont was Ira Allen, Ethan's brother.

However, the Continental Congress refused to recognize Vermont as a state. Its members said that the United States had declared themselves free of Great Britain, but that did not mean that any group inside American territory could declare itself a free state. Congress itself preferred to be the body that determined what would be a state and what would not. Once a state proved that it could run and support itself, it could **petition** Congress for statehood. Because Vermont did not follow the proper procedure, it could not become a state or send representatives to Congress.

But the people of Vermont had already made the decision to become free, and the rulings of Congress could not change their minds about that. Until Vermont became a state in 1791, it was a **republic,** ruled by its own government, not by the United States government.

Ira Allen, Ethan's brother, built this house in the Battenkill Valley of southern Vermont. Ira was the surveyor-general of Vermont.

Confiscating land

When Ethan Allen returned to Vermont, he quickly became involved in politics. Because the trouble with New York over ownership of land in Vermont continued, Vermont set up a special court to oversee these problems. Ethan Allen was put in charge of **confiscating** land from settlers from New York, called "Yorkers" by the people of Vermont, as well as from **Loyalists.** Allen and his men forced Yorkers off their land, then claimed the land for Vermont. To gain favor from American leaders, Allen sometimes gave the land to members of Congress or to officers in the **Continental army.** He simply wrote their names on the new deeds. Often these people did not even realize they owned the land until it was pointed out to them.

Secret negotiations

While Allen was busy protecting the people of Vermont from those who argued against the state's right to exist, he also was dealing with a situation that could have become even more dangerous. The British knew that Vermont had declared itself a state, and that the **Continental Congress** did not recognize it as such. The British also knew that most people in Vermont were frustrated with the refusal of the United States to allow elected representatives from Vermont into Congress. On March 30, 1780, Allen received a letter from British General Beverly Robinson. In the letter, Robinson presented to Allen an idea. He wanted Allen to help reunite America with Great Britain. In return, the British king would make Vermont a favored state. Vermont would become a part of Great Britain, protected by the British army, but would have its own government.

As soon as he received the letter, Allen showed it to the Governor Chittenden of Vermont and a few other people. They all decided that the best thing to do would be not to answer the letter at all. But the governor said that perhaps Vermont could take advantage of Great Britain's willingness to work with them by presenting a deal to Britain. Canada was a part of Great Britain, and some soldiers from Vermont were being held as prisoners of war by the British in Canada. The governor wanted Allen to work out a prisoner exchange like the one that had set Allen free. Allen told the idea to General Frederick Haldimand, the governor of Canada and the commander of British forces

British General Beverly Robinson tried to persuade Allen twice to have Vermont side with the British.

there, but the exchange did not work out. Later, however, Allen met with British Major Carlton, and the two agreed to a truce between Vermont and Great Britain. The truce was kept secret from the United States.

In February, Allen received another letter from General Robinson that again asked Vermont to join the British cause. Allen did not answer this letter, either, but on March 9, 1781, he decided to send both letters to Congress. He enclosed his own letter with them. In it, he said that Vermont had a right to be independent. He added that the British would not have presented this idea to Vermont if Congress had allowed Vermont to join the United States. In his letter, Allen showed how serious he was about Vermont's independence. He wrote, "I am as resolutely determined to defend the independence of Vermont, as Congress are that of the United States; and rather than fail, will retire with hardy Green Mountain Boys, into the desolate caverns of the mountains, and wage war with human nature at large." This incident is often called the Haldimand Affair by historians because it involves Allen's **negotiations** with Haldimand.

Because of his dealings with the British, Allen was charged with **treason** by Congress but later the charges were dropped. When the Revolutionary War ended, so did Allen's negotiations with the British.

Vermont

The name *Vermont* comes from two French words, *vert*, meaning "green," and *mont*, meaning "mountain."

Most historians agree that Allen did not seriously consider Robinson's offer. They say that Allen was using the letter to emphasize Vermont's desire to become part of the United States. He wanted Congress to see that if it would not accept Vermont into the Union, Great Britain was ready to open its arms to Vermont.

By August 1781, some important American leaders, including George Washington, supported the idea of Vermont joining the United States. But many in Congress, especially those from New York, did not agree. Many objected simply because Vermont had not followed the proper procedure to become a state. In 1783 Congress even considered invading Vermont to force its people to give in to New York's demands regarding claims to land. But Washington, who was still commander of the **Continental army,** refused to invade the **republic** and persuaded Congress that the move would not be wise.

The Green Mountains in Vermont are one of the oldest mountain ranges in the United States. When settlers first came to Vermont, the mountains were covered in forests of evergreens. That is how the Green Mountains got their name.

9 Last Years and Legacy

In 1784 Ethan Allen quit politics and retired to his 350-acre (142-hectare) farm in Burlington, Vermont, with his new wife, Frances, also known as Fanny. His first wife, Mary, had died in 1783. Allen and Mary had five children together. With Fanny, he had three more children.

Allen's popularity had faded somewhat when news of his **negotiations** with the British became known. So he walked away from politics and spent most of his time farming. He also went back to studying religion. In 1763 and 1764, he had studied religious ideas with Dr. Thomas Young, a well-educated man who later became a member of the **Continental Congress.** The two had begun to write a book together, but had not finished it. In 1784, Allen decided to finish writing the book, and it was published. Called *Reason the Only Oracle of Man*, the book outlined Allen's religious beliefs. It was **controversial** because it attacked traditional Christianity. In the book, Allen says that such beliefs are **superstition.** He writes that he prefers reason, or logical thinking, to superstition, and that he believes mankind would be better off if everyone did.

Vermont was finally admitted into the United States in 1791, but Allen did not live to see that event. There are two different stories about how he died. One is that on February 12, 1789, he died of a **seizure** while working on his farm. Another story

1784

Allen quits politics, remarries, and settles down to farming and writing; his book *Reason the Only Oracle of Man* is published

1789

Allen dies on February 12

Deism

Ethan Allen may not have called himself a deist, but his writings show that he followed the religious beliefs of those who were. Deists believe that God cannot be discovered through the Bible or other writings. Instead, people can learn who God is only by observing nature and using their minds and reason.

41

Ethan Allen was buried in Burlington, Vermont. Above is an artist's depiction of Allen's grave site.

says that Allen fell off a sleigh while drunk. Allen was given a large military funeral and was buried in the Green Mountain Cemetery in Burlington, Vermont.

Legacy

The state of Vermont owes much to several members of the Allen family, including Ethan Allen. With his Green Mountain Boys, he defended the rights of Vermont's early settlers. Allen instilled a fierce sense of independence in Vermont's citizens—one that they are still proud of today.

Fire destroys books

While Allen's book *Reason the Only Oracle of Man* was controversial and was condemned by many church leaders, few people actually got to read the book. Many of its pages were destroyed by an accidental fire at the office of the book's printer, Mr. Haswell. Later, Haswell purposely burned most of the rest of the copies. No one is sure whether he did this because he did not like the book, but Haswell did join the Methodist Church soon afterward. Today, copies of the book are very hard to find.

Allen studied past deeds and land claims and used his knowledge to help settlers in the New Hampshire Grants and other **colonies.** The many **pamphlets** and books he wrote provide a view of the ideas people had during the Revolutionary era and a history of the times.

Allen also provided a brave example of a rough-and-tumble **frontier** hero when the country desperately needed one. This was shown when, with Benedict Arnold at his side, he stormed the fort at Ticonderoga and claimed it for America. He was an example of bravery and patriotism for the American people when he became a British prisoner of war. He showed the rest of the world just how stubborn and serious Americans were about independence.

Ethan Allen lived in this farmhouse in Burlington, Vermont. It still stands today as a reminder of the huge impact Allen had on the formation of Vermont as a state.

Timeline

January 21, 1738	Ethan Allen is born in Litchfield County, Connecticut (*some sources say 1737*)
Summer 1757	Ethan Allen joins Litchfield County **militia** and marches to Fort William Henry
January 1762	Ethan Allen becomes part owner of an ironworks
June 23, 1762	Marries Mary Brownson
1770	Allen family moves to the New Hampshire Grants; Green Mountain Boys militia formed
1774	Allen's book *A Brief Narrative of the Proceedings of the Government of New York* published
April 19, 1775	Battles at Lexington and Concord, Massachusetts
April 23, 1775	Massachusetts Congress orders thousands of soldiers to Boston
May 10, 1775	Allen and Arnold capture Fort Ticonderoga; the Second **Continental Congress** opens in Philadelphia
May 15, 1775	Arnold captures Fort St. John's; days later, Allen tries to occupy the fort but is chased away by British reinforcements
July 3, 1775	George Washington takes over leadership of the **Continental army**
September 1775	Allen is captured by the British at Montreal and his long captivity begins
December 23, 1775	England's King George III announces that all American **colonies** are closed to trade
March 1776	Cannons taken from Fort Ticonderoga are placed on Dorchester Heights above Boston
May 3, 1776	Allen is released from the British in a prisoner exchange
June 28, 1776	In Charleston, South Carolina, American troops fight off the British
June and July 1776	Thousands of British soldiers, ships, and weapons arrive in New York
July 2, 1776	Congress votes to declare independence from Great Britain
July 4, 1776	Congress adopts the Declaration of Independence
August 1776	Battle of Long Island; Washington's troops are defeated; later, the Americans escape northward
December 24–25, 1776	Washington and his troops cross the Delaware to New Jersey and launch a surprise attack on German forces fighting for the British there; the Germans surrender
January 15, 1777	The New Hampshire Grants declare themselves a free and independent state

July 6, 1777	British General Burgoyne captures Fort Ticonderoga
September 26, 1777	British forces occupy Philadelphia
October 7, 1777	Battle of Saratoga, led by Generals Gates and Arnold
October 17, 1777	General Burgoyne surrenders to General Gates
November 15, 1777	Congress adopts the Articles of Confederation as the nation's new constitution; a constitution outlines the basic beliefs and laws of a nation, the powers and duties of its government, and the rights of its people
February 1778	The French agree to help the United States win the war
July 10, 1778	France declares war against Great Britain
December 29, 1778	The British capture Savannah, Georgia
September— October 1779	Eight hundred Americans are killed in Savannah
December 26, 1779	The British attack Charleston, South Carolina
March 30, 1780	Allen receives the first letter from General Robinson
May 12, 1780	The British capture Charleston
July 11, 1780	Six thousand French soldiers arrive at Newport, Rhode Island
March 9, 1781	Allen sends his letters from Robinson to Congress
August 1, 1781	British General Cornwallis and 10,000 British soldiers arrive in Yorktown, Virginia, to rest
August 30, 1781	A French fleet arrives off Yorktown
September 28, 1781	Washington and American troops begin the **siege** at Yorktown
October 19, 1781	General Cornwallis officially surrenders at Yorktown
November 10, 1782	The last battle of the war is fought in Ohio territory
February 4, 1783	England announces the war is over
1784	Allen quits politics, remarries, and publishes *Reason the Only Oracle of Man*
February 12, 1789	Allen dies

Glossary

ambush surprise attack

boundary division between two spaces, such as between states

brevet colonel military officer with a honorary higher ranking than other colonels

charter written document that outlines the location and boundaries of a city, town, or institution

colonist person who lives in a colony

colony settlement in a new territory that is tied to an established nation

committee of correspondence committee set up during the Revolutionary era to promote communication between the colonies

confiscate seize; take away something by claiming authority to do so

Continental army first official army of the United States; the Continental army was formed in 1775 and was led by George Washington

Continental Congress group of representatives from the American colonies who carried out the duties of the government

controversial causing or related to controversy, a long or heated discussion about something that people have a great difference of opinion about

desert escape military duty without permission

evict force out, sometimes using physical force

forge furnace where iron ore is made soft so it can be made into various forms

French and Indian War fought between Great Britain and France in the northern American colonies from 1756 to 1763; some Native Americans fought with the French, while others fought with the British

frontier border between two countries; edge of the settled part of a country

harass continually annoy

Loyalist someone who remains loyal to a particular cause; during the American Revolution, a loyalist was someone who remained loyal to Great Britain

militia citizens banded together in a military unit; members of a militia are called militiamen

musket firearm with a long barrel

negotiation process of discussion and compromise with another party to achieve a goal

pamphlet booklet with no cover, usually made of paper folded into smaller parts

Parliament supreme lawmaking body in Great Britain

parole during a prison term, a release with certain conditions

Patriot person who supports his or her country; during the American Revolution, those who fought for freedom from Great Britain

petition apply for formally, in a written document

recruit find new members; one of those new members is called a recruit

reinforcements fresh additions, such as fresh troops

republic government with an elected head, such as a president, and in which citizens vote for representatives who make laws

schooner ship with two masts

seizure sudden attack

siege surround an opposing army and capture it by bombing and blockading it

sloop boat with one mast and one sail

superstition beliefs or practices resulting from ignorance, fear of the unknown, or trust in magic or chance

survey find out the size, shape, or position of, as in an area of land

tactic method

taunt insult

tavern building in which alcoholic beverages are sold; in colonial times, taverns were more like inns, where alcoholic beverages and food were sold and rooms were rented out

treason attempt to overthrow the government one lives under

Further Reading

Anderson, Dale. *The American Revolution.* Chicago: Raintree, 2003.

Hossell, Karen Price. *The Boston Tea Party: Rebellion in the Colonies.* Chicago: Heinemann Library, 2003.

Isaacs, Sally Senzell. *America in the Time of George Washington (1747–1803).* Chicago: Heinemann Library, 1999.

Smolinski, Diane. *Important People of the Revolutionary War.* Chicago: Heinemann Library, 2001.

Smolinski, Diane. *Land Battles of the Revolutionary War.* Chicago: Heinemann Library, 2001.

Index